A View From an Empty Nest,

With Only a Few Ruffled Feathers

Poetic Reflections on the Family

by

Alisa B. Bates

Dedication

This book is dedicated to my amazing family.

You have filled our home with love and laughter for 39 years,

providing a plethora of life's lessons and experiences.

I have been blessed with

the joys of motherhood

and a truly awesome husband.

Contents

Introduction

Faded Wedding Pictures

The waistlines have thickened, the hairlines have thinned.
Wrinkles now settle where dimples once grinned.
The man at my side not so thin or so young,
his hands scarred and calloused from the work that they've done.
The sacred promises agreed to that day
have not been neglected, in fact, I can say,
through the struggles, blessings, and children we've had,
we've shared happy moments and learned from the sad.
Sometimes it's important to stop and admit
when the old-fashioned wedding gown doesn't quite fit,
the diamond ring has been missing for ages,
and faded pictures rest beneath yellowed pages,
that's when the same couple who has withstood the weather,
realizes they've grown in love with each other.

(Faded Wedding Pictures, by Alisa B. Bates, used by permission
of the Ensign Magazine© By Intellectual Reserve, Inc.)

Field Dance

Missing Piece

I heard your voice

and instantly knew

you were the one.

From the corner shadows,

I memorized your expression,

thrilled that the voice

owned an intriguing face.

I knew I would never love again,

would not be whole

would not grow old

without you,

though we had never met.

All I had left to do

was convince you.

Discovery

Do not live with your eyes focused too far ahead,

For the most precious things are within your reach...

...waiting to be discovered.

Bonding

Alone we are nothing...

But together we create a love so strong

We could ignite the universe.

A Near-Perfect Union

Welcome to my world...

> Where life is full of song.

> Each hour is full of meaning.

> We'll be joyful all day long.

Welcome to my life...

> Where so much is held in store,

> Where dreams become reality,

> It's clear what life is for.

Welcome to my soul...

> Where my genuine feelings start,

> Where sincere secrets are guarded...

...Welcome to my heart.

Nesting

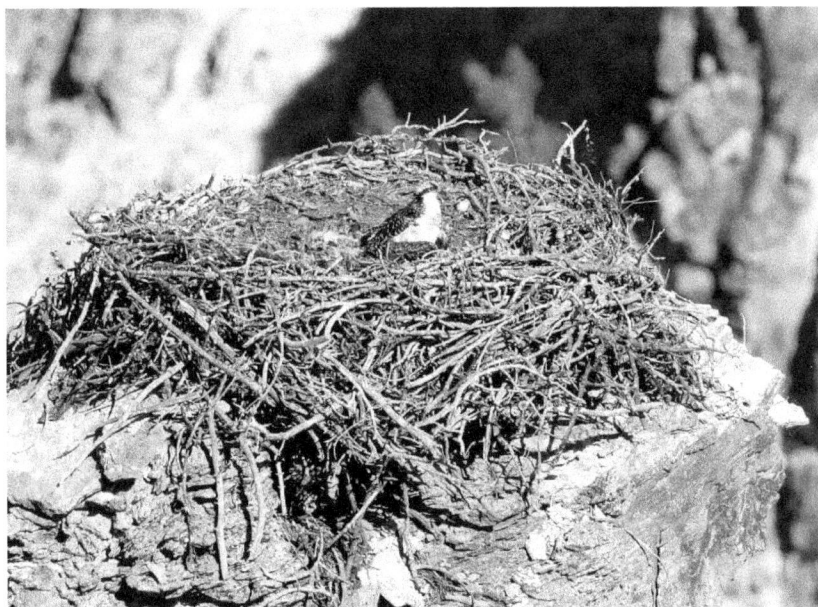

First Child

From the moment they placed you against me,

I felt your trust

and shuddered.

Could I do it right?

Suddenly I felt young, gangly,

a baby myself,

trusted by God to take you in my arms,

in my home

and hold you,

mold you,

into a man of God.

The burden seemed tough,

Incomprehensible,

but it wasn't my burden alone.

Your father stood near,

shouldering the responsibility,

while our Heavenly Father

delivered strength and direction.

After all, you were His, before you were ours.

When Baby Smiles

When baby smiles,

the wilted rosebud blooms again.

When baby smiles,

the rainbow takes the place of rain.

The lion and the lamb embrace,

troubles flee without a trace,

the world becomes a cheerful place,

When baby smiles.

Natural Light

No ocean flows more freely, than a mother's love.

No wave more joyous, painful, or fonder

Will linger with you longer

For there is nothing stronger-

Than a mother's love.

No Spaniel stays as loyal, as a mother's heart.

Whichever pathway you choose to take

Whatever decisions you choose to make

There is no heart easier to cheer, or break-

Than a mother's heart.

No songbird's song is more sincere, than a mother's prayer.

No prayer touches Heaven more sweetly

Or desires an answer more completely

Nor is full of gratitude as neatly-

As a mother's prayer.

No sunbeam lifts you higher, than a mother's soul.

She will cheer for you, hope for you

Fear for you, mope for you

There is an endless support for you

In a mother's soul.

No show-horse cadence matches a mother's intuition.

Seldom a secret you can keep

She may be nudged in thought or sleep

The mother-child connection runs that deep-

Through a mother's intuition.

No rose petal is as tender, as a mother's touch.

She is blossoming near to share your load

As you struggle down life's hectic road

You will always find a hand to hold-

In a mother's touch.

No lighthouse beams as brightly, as a mother's hope.

Showering hope and faith for as long as she lives

Her heart will be the first to forgive

Her face will shine; life will be fine-

With a mother's hope.

No homecoming will be dearer, than in a mother's arms.

She welcomed your life, while risking her own

Nurtured you from the time you were born

You will eternally be accepted at home-

And in your mother's arms.

First Mother

Eve-

Woman in a new world to bring to life,

Planting gardens and creating a home,

Loving your children,

Holding them close,

And praying they would be righteous spirits.

Sorrow must've gripped your heart

With tightly clenched fists

As you watched them growing,

And bringing the first sins upon this earth.

What a joy Abel must've been

Never losing his childish innocence,

Loving God, his family -and you.

The first murder-

That of your faithful son

Must've been inconceivable,

As the world had never witnessed murder before-

More so as his murderer was Cain,

Your own flesh and blood,

Whom you had taught, loved and hoped for.

But God, knowing you needed healing sent Seth,

Another very righteous mortal to you to find joy in-

A child who glorified his Father in Heaven.

Eve-

Still we look to you who had unbearable sorrows

And shattered dreams,

Yet still remained faithful, joyful and strong,

An example to us as the first wife,

The first children's influence, teacher, and mother.

?

The six-inch scar

Shaped like a question mark

Symbolizes the question:

"Will she walk again?"

A skilled physician

Surgically tore a knee apart

And pieced it back together,

His hands guided by God.

God heals a crippled mother.

Rising from her bed she walks,

Ready and willing

To raise children unto Him.

The wound is sealed

A scar revealed,

Physical evidence

Of God's love

Without question.

Hatching

Boy to Man

Blonde boy, big smile

crawling through Joshua's Arch,

chasing lizards, tickling ladybugs.

With pistol dangling from your eyelid,

or wadding paper up your nose,

I could kiss away your tears,

silence all your fears,

but I never learned

to call back the years.

Grown man, loving father,

rainbow trout fishing with your kids,

tossing and cooing with wee ones,

creating memories,

building trust.

Kiss away their tears,

Silence all their fears,

for you'll never learn

to call back the years.

Recovery

Silence-

    Fills the halls

    and quiets the saddened house.

Only the rumble of the upper apartment vacuum

    breaks the stillness

    as I lay heavy-hearted in my bed.

Where is the scamper of little feet,

    the clicking of the baby swing,

    the happy sound of children's laughter

    or even the shrillness of their childish cries?

Am I a stranger in my own home,

    unable to exist without the whining,

    the dirty diapers,

    the teddy bears,

    and the lullabies?

Only a few short hours ago

    I was welcomed from the hospital with squeals

    cheerful eyes and slobbers.

Now, Grandma has the treasures,

       leaving me with the memories

       and a tear-streaked pillow.

I wipe my eyes,

       yank the covers over my head and begin-

       to face the lonely days of

Recovery.

Piano Student

His long narrow fingers,

that bulge at the knuckles,

glide gracefully across each octave,

while his head and shoulders

bob rhythmically.

His love of music,

passed down through generations,

is woven into each measure.

Dressed in a white shirt

and crimson tie,

this handsome musician

fills our Sunday afternoon

with a stirring rendition of

"Oh, My Father."

Beneath his right eye

a childhood scar,

resembling a smile,

matches the grin on my face

as I, his teacher, his mother,

recognize talent

that has surpassed my own.

Stillness

The sun lowers in the sky, filtering pale orange light

between the branches of the towering green ash

that looms above your headstone.

Tonight the cemetery is quiet, serene,

with silence broken

only by the rustling of leaves in the breeze

and the songs of warblers and lark sparrows

perched in the trees on this peaceful bluff.

Cut flowers, potted mums, and spinning pinwheels

decorate your sacred spot,

where I have placed pink rosebuds

and warm teardrops for 35 years.

Photos of bygone years

capture my change in countenance

after my heart was touched and forever altered.

Though yours was a life unlived,

life, for me,

took on greater value

and a yearning to reunite family.

How I miss the child I never knew,

but love dearly,

and desire to meet again:

"Our Sweet, Angel Baby, Emily."

The Continuous Diet

Along with each baby comes more weight to loose.

This is the source of my post-partum blues.

I exercise and diet to reach the goal that I've set

but muscle strains and hunger pains are all that I get.

When finally my denims are loosening a bit

I'm expecting again and the diet must quit.

With the birth of my last baby it all started once more—

the struggle to become the weight that I was YEARS before.

As I tell my plans to my husband he snickers and grins

Because my new "baby" turned out to be twins – Again.

Biology Meets History

Leaping up the concrete steps,

taking two at a time,

my son flings the wooden door open

and brilliantly proclaims-

"It's an archival treasure!"

He snaps open

a "Modern Biology" book,

found in the school's 'free' bin.

His banana smile splits apart,

revealing perfect teeth.

He flips through the pages

and layered transparencies

of frog guts.

I recognize the frog from my past

and grab the book.

Suddenly, I am seventeen,

boy crazy in biology,

too squeamish to dissect frogs,

too naive to ponder

the chapter on twins.

I search his olive green eyes

with the blazing yellow rings,

the same eyes that reflect

from my own bathroom mirror.

There's a chapter on that as well.

As he snatches the book back,

our hands nearly touch,

our generations nearly connect.

Uneven

Long, bony fingers

skip up and down the neck

of the ivory guitar,

electrifying audiences.

A determined attitude,

a skilled surgeon

and a miraculous blessing,

healed and regenerated

his routered off fingertip.

Battling opposition,

this musician is proficient.

Lips pursed, focusing,

hair flipping,

knees dipping,

feet shuffling,

his music jolts

like the lightning bolt

on his black guitar strap.

Grand Finale

Blasting fireworks splash the sky.

Fiery reds, shimmering blues,

bursting into glittery fountains.

Trickling slowly,

sizzling out,

one at a time.

In grand finale, the last two rockets

shoot upward, explode together,

reflecting iridescent light

in the silent lake below.

Drizzling,

fizzling,

dark.

ROY G BIV

Driving Ridge Road in pouring rain,

wiper blades streak the glass

in clumsy cadence.

Struggling with vision

through foggy windshield,

I become anxious.

Rain tempers to a drizzle,

rainbow stretches across gray sky.

Vision clearing, heart rejoicing:

The rainbow points to my front door!

Hastily, I pursue the pot of gold.

Treasured loved ones await.

Fledging

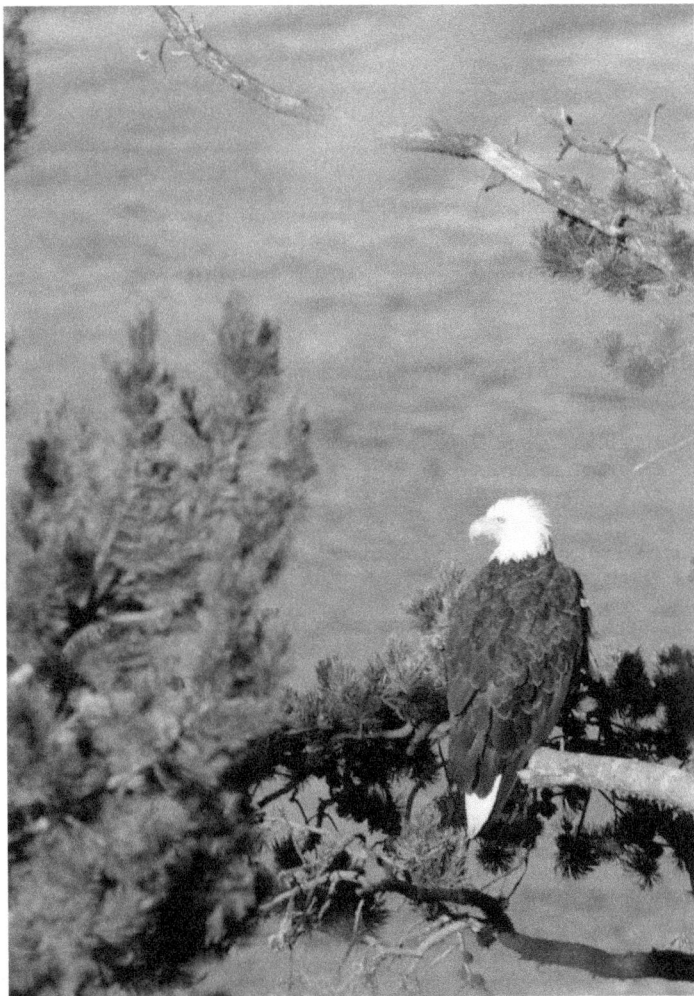

Fledgling

Mother coaxes her eaglet towards the nest's edge,

Though longing to nurture; she knows he must fledge.

Both eagles hesitate, knowing they must try.

She must learn to let go; he must learn to fly.

Toppling from the nest he falls amidst the trees,

Spreading his young wings, he grasps a gentle breeze.

Swept upward through the clouds and into the blue,

Soaring, gliding, as God intended him to.

On coral cliff his majestic shadow cast,

Drifting above willow and sage canyon vast.

She watches her fledgling calmly hovering,

Awaiting cliffs she'll soon be discovering.

Baby Steps

I watched a young mother ...

Encouraging her son's first steps.

Clutching his mother's fingers, teetering,

fearful to let go.

Looking up at his mother, he yearned to say –

"I'm not ready! Please, give me more time!"

His mother urged him,

like I did - in years past,

until I experienced how hastily flee

those tender moments of childhood.

I watch you, my precious child...

Eagerly taking your next steps.

I long to cling to you tightly and say-

"I'm not ready! Please, just a little more time!"

But something whispers "Let go." And so...

As you move forward, I'll be ready

when you call, when you fall, or for any reason at all.

Please, forgive me if I teeter,

or brush a straying tear

in these fearful, adapting moments of motherhood.

Leap and We'll See

Little Nanny Two Shoes,

in the green alpine sweater,

plopped into my lap,

and wrapped her arms around my neck.

Rocking on the edge of her bed,

we sang "Angel Friends."

A surprise tender moment,

with my college student.

Tears puddled in her eyes.

Feeling the winds of change,

she was afraid.

As we rocked, I listened,

not only to her words,

but to the whisperings I felt.

My mind flashed -

back to the days of the 'pop-pop' shirt

and camping at Mirror Lake,

back to the 'clack-clack' shoes

dancing on our kitchen floor.

When Clinny arrived in his white Topaz,

I knew that her prince had come.

She was finally complete.

From "Leap and we'll see" to...

"For all Eternity."

Teenage Attitude

"I'll do what I want!"

Bumbling, hoping to escape

Life's consequences.

"All Missionaries Accounted For"

Rocks tumbled upon you.

A trembling wall crashed into bits

around your head.

Safely, I slept: 5000 miles away.

TV stations reported the quake.

Pushing the worry to a back shelf of my mind,

I dropped to my knees and prayed for angels,

not knowing they had already come-

familiar angels from Heaven

and loving earthly heroes in God's service.

Remembering your smile,

the sunlight that brightens my soul,

sparked faith and hope in my heart.

Hearing of the miracles, I prayed again.

This time in gratitude.

Your injuries healed, your precious life spared.

God rescued my son: His missionary.

I prayed the experience would not change you.

But it did.

Your soul awakened to God's love for you.

Sweet Music

Blonde beauty on horseback

Belting out "The Star-Spangled Banner."

Red sequined jacket, black felt hat.

A big voice in a small package.

Youthful sweetheart in church

Soloing "If the Savior Stood Beside Me."

Scarlet sweater, floral skirt.

Touching hearts and souls.

Spunky soprano in Vocal Jazz

Hamming up "Rays Rock House."

Periwinkle vest, black bow tie.

Playfully dancing on stage.

Mo Tab lilts from my stereo

Performing "For the Beauty of the Earth."

I picture her, in blue velvet gown,

Joyfully resonating with the All-State choir.

Sometimes, in quiet moments-

I still hear her singing.

Scrapbooking

His slender face graces the pages

of my photo albums.

His two blackened eyes, blue football helmet,

and family vacations.

Recently your face shows up beside his.

Your Eternal marriage, holiday fun.

More pages to add

containing your smile.

Now his face fills your scrapbook.

Precious photos cropped, pasted,

and set into pages,

As you create memories together.

Empty Nest

Patchwork

We are different, each of us,

like fabric in a patchwork quilt,

stitched together to create

the unique family that we are.

Each block differs from the rest

adding pops of color and touches of texture

to the final product.

Spiritual binding unites us,

completes us,

and keeps us from fraying along the edges.

Together, through eternity, we shall be –

Patchwork Friends.

Kitchen Table

Bought for convenience this old kitchen table,

Picnic style with benches,

Has seated an array of children,

Without having to fumble with chairs.

It has been used for eating, playing,

Education and family parties.

Our son once refurbished it

Fulfilling a Scout assignment,

Which brought new life to the table.

It bears signs of wear

But remains beautiful to us.

The family of nine living at home

Has whittled down to two.

Retired and elderly,

Remembering the hectic, exciting days

When these benches were filled.

We will replace it

When the heirloom table bequeathed to us,

Finds its way into our home.

Our table will likely be passed down then as well.

Family members are like kitchen tables,

We treasure them,

Spend beautiful moments with them

And refurbish them when needed.

As they begin to wear out

We fear life without them.

When that day comes

Their beauty is enhanced by rich memories

To be passed down through generations.

New Grandson

Hearing your first squeaks,

I nuzzle you against my shoulder.

Your flashing obsidian eyes

memorize my face.

I sing to my blue flannel angel friend.

Puckered lips part, twist,

and release a pale pink tongue

in response.

I brush a sudsy sponge

across orange-red skin

and dark hair tipped in gold.

So pure is Heaven's recent resident.

Serenely you bask

in the lavender luminescent bili lights,

as if accustomed to such radiance.

Your own radiance reflects His love.

Space Cadet

Launched into Grandma's house,

like a steely ball in a pinball game.

His luminous eyes

resemble full moons,

waning into crescents

when he blinks.

He misses nothing,

except a step on the staircase.

As he bumps the wall,

two pictures plummet.

Lunar storms flood my shoulder.

Buzz Lightyear comforts.

Darting from my arms,

he empties two toy boxes.

Salt is shaken

onto the floor.

Stealing a pumpkin loaf,

he hides beneath the table.

He's caught in the act.

Spitting crumbs, he shouts

"Grandpa is a dumb name!"

He reels in a green seal,

barbecues it and serves it

with hot chocolate.

Cuddling together on my lap,

we read *Thomas the Train*.

Outside, the moon rises in night sky,

Inside, moon child whispers "Goodbye."

Sleepy eyes wax and wane.

Grandma cuddles him,

hesitant to let go.

Points tallied, high score!

Game over.

Let's play again soon.

(Published under first publication rights in the Jan-Feb 2009 issue of Mothering magazine.)

Zoom Out

I nearly stepped on it-

while photographing the reflection of Majestic Mountain in

the still, green waters of Boldger Reservoir.

Stopping, stooping,

you knelt beside it. Several small flowers, clustered on a

ragged-leafed plant.

Tenderly,

you touched a bloom, and rubbed it between your short,

chubby fingers.

Leaning closer,

I studied each purplish, spindly petal around a mustard yellow
center,

through your three-year-old eyes,

from behind a 55 mm zoom lens.

I stood up

and removed the camera from my eyes.

The whole valley was dotted with pale purple asters.

Funny, I hadn't noticed them before.

Mid-Life Crisis

Candy apple red aero

Shoots down highway 6.

I hang tightly to my man.

The wind whips my hair;

Gnats collect in my teeth.

If it doesn't kill me,

The ride will thrill me,

Until Honda bills me.

Crossing Over

Blaring horn, blinding light

my heart jumped.

Freaking out,

clawing your arm,

I caused you to lose control.

The Honda 750

slid and swerved.

Horrified, mortified,

I trusted you.

Don't let us crash!

Peeling out, spinning off

the hot iron rails

and rickety ties.

Miraculously,

the threatening train thundered safely behind us.

Balancing Act

The sleek, black seal

performs in the center ring,

rhythmically juggling

two colorful beach balls

on its slippery snout.

Lifting its front flippers

to applaud itself,

both balls bounce to the floor.

Lunging forward to rescue the balls

the seal flops flat on its face.

Who's Stalking Who?

Mighty in stature; sleek body, matted cape

sharp horns upon his monstrous head,

the bison bull grazed in the blue bunch grasses.

Billy sped up the muddy path to photograph him.

I plodded along behind.

Another bull, in a neighboring meadow,

came into view.

Billy spotted it, changed focus,

and stepped stealthily toward this bull

for a close - range picture.

The first bull, spotting Billy,

slowly stepped toward him.

He did not see it approaching.

My yell, or warning,

would cause the bull to charge.

I silently, prayerfully, watched.

A shudder ran up my spine.

The animal crept closer, closer-

eyes focused upon him!

A ponderosa pine bough snapped.

Man and beast beheld each other,

from only a few feet away.

Man backed off a little...

...after pausing to take a few fantastic photos.

He deserved it - in the end -

Billy wanted a close-up shot,

and that's exactly what he got!

Ursa Major

Black Bear brawling at twilight.

We wake in cold, clammy sweats.

Calm now, no worries today,

He's miles away.

Attacking family and friends.

Poison tracks imprint our souls.

Lurking near our Dogwood tree,

He's stalking me.

Chasing, chomping at my heels.

Crimson blood soaks white stockings.

Fight back with empty hand kicks,

Cheap parlor tricks.

Sear him with a blazing torch.

Great Hunter's arrows pierce him.

The savage battle begins,

Nobody wins.

Dance beneath Big Dipper's gaze.

Reach for a glimpse of heaven.

Hope whispers in a child's eyes,

Kolob's Grand prize.

Ursa Minor

Black bear, kicked, bruised, defeated,

lumbers back into the woods

licking his empty black paws,

grieving his lost cause.

Colored leaves wither and fade,

but cling to the maple trees.

Nuts and seeds will satisfy

until his next try.

He casts a glance at the town

that violently cast him out.

A dark, dank cave holds his fate.

Crawling inside, he'll hibernate.

Our greatest fears diminish.

Peaceful dreams replace nightmares.

We praise God in thanksgiving.

Joyously living.

Empty Nest Christmas

Slowly, waking from a peaceful night's sleep

Void of tiny tots' giggles and floorboards that creak.

No trumpets blaring or jingle bells ringing,

No "Hallelujah" shouts or opera singing.

This year, no alarms were set under our bed.

No prank calls in the wee hours. We slept in instead.

We didn't set traps to keep them from the tree.

I woke up this morning to catch you staring at me.

As it should be, I suppose, with families of their own,

Why, it's just you and me, Love, our fledglings have flown.

Unrushed, we unwrap gifts; carols play on CD

Then read scriptural accounts of the nativity.

Still, Christmas Eve dinner was hectic with faces aglow

The chaotic Nativity play didn't quite flow.

New Christmas traditions; let's enjoy every minute.

French toast with our son's family will begin it.

Driving slick roads to visit each pajama-clad child

Hugs, squeals of joy, and show -n- tell make it worthwhile.

Amidst noise and toys filling each home to the brim,

I find myself pondering, reflecting on Him.

It must please Him as families gather in His name

Remembering Him, the Savior who long-ago came

Bringing light, endless love, joy and hope to the sinner.

Now it's time we sit down, to a simple Christmas dinner.

Warm wishes shared with each family member,

Create new Christmas traditions to remember.

Sitting by firelight, eating turtles, you and me,

Christmas, this year, was just as it should be.

Ruffled Feathers

Taming White Water

Angry water cuts like a knife

Through the verdant meadows of life

And travels in one direction.

Leap the stream while the flow is light

Before the water rises high

And the current whirls you away.

Raft the river near sunset's glow

Before the tamarisk trees grow

While the water lilies are young.

Sail that lake to the other side

Drop that burden; swallow that pride

For you cannot bridge an ocean.

Bull in a China Shop

My aunt's elegant mansion,

filled with as many rooms as she had grandchildren,

was ornately decorated

with rubies, gold, diamonds and pearls.

Visiting the mansion, my mom admired

shimmering chandeliers, tasseled draperies,

and porcelain vases from the orient.

The caretaker,

in honor of her grandmother's memory,

dusted, polished, and preserved

the mansion in pristine condition.

A Spanish fighting bull, charged in

shredding the foreign tapestries with his pointy horns,

crashing into crystal cruses and jade dragons,

shattering fine china into a million pieces.

The caretaker shrieked in horror.

Immediately the brown bull halted, stamped,

and turned to face my mother.

As Mom wept bitterly,

he mockingly, thrust back his mighty head

and laughed,

puffing fire from his nostrils.

Whipping his horns, leaving wreckage in his path,

the bull bolted back through the mansion

and out through the door in which he entered.

The mansion lay in ruin.

And great was the fall thereof.

Upper Shelf

Your sparked anger, silent and spoken,

cuts like a crystal vase that has been broken,

agony oozing from an opened scar,

fading light bleeding from a wishing star.

Capturing the pain as a puddle catches rain.

It's too hard to believe; I won't wear it on my sleeve.

I'll hide it in the corner of an upper shelf

locked in a box of secrets about myself-

The mistakes, the heartaches,

don't know how many more of those I can take.

Hidden snares, awkward stares,

the times I have been taken unawares.

Splashing tears in the shower,

draining my strength and my power,

more nightmares than daydreams,

more gray areas than white, it seems.

I need flowery flip flops

to squish out the drip drops - this spring-

A friendly face, a peaceful place,

the healing power of a warm embrace.

Peeking through crumpled blinds,

Waiting for the sun to shine.

Well, you can't blame me.

You can't shame me.

I can do that all by myself.

Tower of Bricks

A white, colonial house

built on a tower of bricks

overlooked the city.

From my window,

I saw the tower teetering.

Right, then left

Picking up speed.

No earthquake to cause it,

no breeze to propel it,

just swaying on its own above the city.

Will it fall? I wondered.

Should I send for help?

Surely someone else has called.

As I watched,

the house dipped low,

then toppled to the ground,

splattering into pieces.

The woman inside of it died.

No one saved her.

Implosion

The ground beneath our house moaned and groaned

and shook like sifted flour.

I paused a moment, not knowing what was going on.

You grabbed my hand, and together we started to run.

I paused again, wondering what earthly possession

I could save.

You shook your head, encouraging me to leave behind

everything we owned.

We stood outside of the house

and watched it crumble.

Pieces flew everywhere,

as the ground swallowed up our home.

Helpless, hopeless,

all we could do was watch.

We stood there,

with nothing but the pajamas on our backs

and each other.

Winds of Change

The winds of change rustled as I was taken

from the wooden shelf.

I felt the cuts as my lengthy vines were shortened.

Brown, brittle leaves were rubbed off.

When my very roots were exposed and shaken

I held on, gripping the life that was left in me.

Would I ever recover?

I plead for help, but feared no one heard.

Slowly, gently, I was placed in a fine, new pot.

Fresh soil was poured around me.

A gentle hand, pushed and patted the dirt,

providing comfort and cushioning to my shaken roots.

Healthy food and drink energized my soul.

A soothing shower sprinkled my parched leaves.

Soon, I was replaced to the sunny shelf.

I stretched out,

discovering more room for my healing roots.

Funny, I hadn't noticed the draining weight

of my lengthy vines,

or the crispy leaves clinging lifelessly.

How long had my roots been entangled

inside my confining pot?

Softly, I breathe. The terror is over.

Growth is certain now.

Already my leaves are lifting,

and leaning towards His light.

What's In Your Backpack?

Stop, drop and roll away

your cumbersome pack,

over the scenic edge

of that rocky track.

For if you lug the load

up the rugged height,

It will jump out and eat you,

bite by venomous bite.

Sunset

A setting sun marks an ending

Not only to laughter but to sorrow.

Its faithful presence whispers peace

and the promise of a new tomorrow.

Soaring

Seasons

If you and I had camped together,

before the babies came,

would we have danced in a meadow,

hiked mountain paths,

or sung beneath the Sprouting moon?

You and I camped with the kids,

stringing wiggly worms on hooks,

waving marshmallow torches,

picking Utah Firecracker

and howling at the Strawberry moon.

Now, you and I camp with the grandkids,

chasing lizards into crevices,

digging dirt with plastic shovels,

roasting s'mores in an evening campfire,

and strolling in the light of the Sturgeon moon.

Soon, you and I will camp together,

in a log cabin in the spruces,

dabbling in poetry,

photographing rock squirrels,

hiding from the mystic glow of a Hunter's moon.

Dusk

Please don't forget me, dear,

as grayness and wrinkles come

and memory wanes.

For even the distant moon

reflects in a darkened lake.

Museum Piece

We left the car show, to check out the museum.

Horns blew, lights flashed,

as electric trains slowly climbed mountains,

gaining speed as they rumbled down,

just as the trains of my youth.

"Why is there a hole in that desk?"

The blonde boy holding my hand asked.

"It held an ink bottle so the children could write."

"Did you use one?"

"No, but I saw one in our janitor's closet."

"Oh! Ted and Sally books!

I learned to read from the last editions."

"Adding machines?

My Uncle Bill used one in the old candy store.

Calculators replaced those."

My eyes popped! My jaw dropped!

My high school yearbook rested on a dusty shelf!

Whipping through the pages,

I found my young face!

"Who is that?" the blonde boy asked.

My husband laughed:

"Your Grandma was so young!"

When did my yearbook

become a museum piece?

When did I become a relic?

I pointed out electric typewriters,

cloth diapers and other items I used.

"33 records? Yes, dear.

Someday I'll play one for you."

"Grandma!" he blurted. "Your life is a museum!"

Funny, I mused, in the mirror that night,

how long have I ignored the dip above my lip,

labeled the crow's feet 'smile lines',

and denied that my recent blonding

is really a redhead's gray?

I longed to hold my children, and say:

Enjoy your youth! Cherish your children!

Embrace spiritual blessings!

My mother's voice echoed through the years.

 I hadn't listened – until I met my face...

...Grinning from a museum yearbook.

Crossword Puzzle

Filling in the names of our great greats,

labeling photos and entering dates,

Solving the mystery

of our family history.

Gathering glimpses of long ago-

A proposal letter to Mishy from Joe,

a quilt stitched by Grandma Jane,

A vase belonging to Rosilla Thayn.

Compiling biographies

and faith promoting stories

grandparents will be remembered

through this eternal crossword.

Mom's efforts are appreciated

...on both sides of the veil...

My Sister, How I've Missed Her

"I knew your sister," she softly whispered

in the temple lobby. "No,"

perhaps you knew one of my brothers.

I had two about your age."

She insisted she knew my older sister.

I wish I'd known that bouncy child,

that grinning, chubby-legged angel

with saucer-sized eyes, my only sister

who returned to heaven too soon.

Though I've never met her, I've missed her

dimpled cheeks and curly brown hair

framed within the family album.

Black and white memories of giggling while yanking

my brother's thick red curls. I've listened

longingly to the memories of her young life

and tragic death.

In tender moments, when the veil is thin,

I've welcomed her sweet, sustaining spirit,

like loving arms wrapped around me.

Someday, through sacred eternal covenants,

I will meet my sister.

Silently, They Rolled Away

Where was the band as they left this fair land,

Or the 21 gun salute?

Where was the standing ovation for service and dedication,

Or the Bishop dressed in his suit?

Did I miss the parade and the honoring accolades?

One hundred balloons were not released in the breeze.

Where was the fanfare from friends everywhere,

Or a police escort for citizens such as these?

Where was the hurrah and the hullaballoo?

When did the fat lady sing?

For all of the years, of blood sweat and tears,

It didn't even feel like spring.

Out with the old, in with the new

But no strain of Auld Lang Syne.

I was left with no other, than my friend- my big brother

And pain in this heart of mine.

Open arms will hold them and loving hearts enfold them-

Family waits at the end of the line.

They will laugh and rejoice, with Dale's booming voice,

As they welcome those dear parents of mine.

Do You Still Remember?

Pouring rain, pounds my blue metal roof.

This storm started brewing when you left.

A shiver runs through my soul,

A chill that will only remain cold

Without you.

Crashing thunder, rumbles through the sky,

Startling me, frightening me.

Lurking fears crush heavily in my chest.

Life is cruel and threatening

Without you.

Bolts and jolts of jarring lightning

Eerily spark the evening blackness

Striking a grieving heartache

which refuses to be relieved

Without you.

The lights suddenly douse; darkness fills the house.

Clumsily creeping, warily reaching,

Fumbling, grasping to find my way,

Yet knowing there is no way

Without you.

Seeping, dripping, the ceiling leaks-

Leaking out the tears and fears buried inside

And this sickening sorrow I hide.

There is no comfort, love or peace

Without you.

Mustering hope that the sun will shine again

I smother grief and torrential pain,

Craving your face and tender embrace

Picturing your return to me, that forever I will be

With you.

TWD

A lovely, young, newlywed couple

drive a refurbished Datsun

down a charming, flowery, one lane, mountain path,

eyes aglow, holding hands.

In an instant, the couple becomes middle aged,

driving their Honda Accord along Highway 6.

Texting, looking down, eyes off the road

for only a split second.

The driver misses a turn.

The car flies off of a rocky slope.

Down,

     down,

seemingly in slow motion.

Aspens leaves below become closer and closer.

The car rolls in the grass, rolls again,

then lies silently near White River

at the bottom of the ravine.

The wife moans, awakening gradually, stunned.

The man she loves is unresponsive.

"Wake up! Wake up! It can't end like this!"

Shrieking, trembling, tears streaming, she prays.

"I love you! You can't leave me!"

She takes his dear face into her hands-

The face she has treasured for 36 years.

Slowly, confused, he opens his eyes

to gaze into the face of the sweet love of his life.

As relief replaces fear,

she strokes his face affectionately.

Revision

I created a beautiful poem,

Cut the unimportant words

And all that remained was

"You."

Letting Go

A sweet benefit of Alzheimer's is...

forgetting...

...Now you no longer harbor the guilt.

Mountain Pine

The air is chilly.

Fresh snow blankets distant mountains.

Sunset yellows the lifting clouds.

Cold droplets seep into my bark.

Soon the roar of the falls will be silenced.

The stream will turn to ice.

I shiver. Will I gain another ring?

How long will this crevice support my roots,

before the rock splits and I crash?

I have survived blizzards, violent winds,

and a four ring drought

which left many needles brittle and brown.

During one tempestuous storm,

I gave support to the tree beside me.

Still, I embrace her.

We have withstood brutal storms.

A low branch stretches across the rock,

seeking reflection in the pool.

I stifle the urge to call it back.

Happily, I provide seeds and shelter

to cottontail rabbits,

red squirrels,

and black-capped chickadees.

My needles reach skyward.

Unfinished

How often have I flipped to the last page of a novel eager to find out how it all ends? Now, today, I yearn to turn to the last page of my own book of life, to discover my happy ending.

I'll skim over the death, take a peek at who comes to the funeral, but delve right into the way the story ends. Does it all come together? Do the wrinkles iron out? Are there dog-eared pages of cherished memories?

I hope I took the time to notice the fragrant alyssum on evening walks, bike ride our ballpark route, watch the sand-hill cranes picking seeds from the neighbor's fields, nibble a chocolate chip cookie along with the grandkids, discover the nest of yellow tanangers that flit near the barn, and run my fingers along my newly restored piano.

There's still time to roast a few more marshmallows around a smoldering campfire, sing Christmas carols with the family, enjoy a million hugs and kisses from precious grandchildren, visit mountains, deserts, and far away cities with Billy, and relish in numerous backyard barbecues.

Sprinkled within the chapters of this well-written novel, I am confident I will find treasured moments with my husband and children, both in individual family units and in gyms bulging at the seams with loved ones, united. I long to discover a framed, family photo hanging on a now empty wall.

Those last pages are blank. The work continues. Though unwritten, I hope the ending paragraph reads: She left this earth peacefully, for each family member knew and felt of her Eternal love for them.

And if it does, my life will have been a complete success, and I will be ready to begin the next volume.

Alisa B. Bates

Special Thanks and Photo Credits given to:

Bill Bates

Cover Photo
kon/Shutterstock.com

Field Dance
BGSmith/Shutterstock.com

Hatching
efirm/Shutterstock.com

Additional Reading by Author:

Awaking the Hero

Fox in the Closet

Website: www.alisabbates.com

CPSIA information can be obtained
at www.ICGtesting.com
Printed in the USA
BVHW040232050920
588203BV00018B/1895

9 781546 626039